OUR BIG HOME
An Earth Poem

By Linda Glaser
Art by Elisa Kleven

MILLBROOK PRESS MINNEAPOLIS

To the children, all the children, who will someday
be the caretakers of our big home.
                                    —LG and EK

Text copyright © 2000 by Linda Glaser
Art copyright © 2000 by Elisa Kleven

Millbrook Press
A division of Lerner Publishing Group, Inc.
241 First Avenue North
Minneapolis, Minnesota 55401 U.S.A.

Website address: www.lernerbooks.com

Library of Congress Cataloging-in-Publication Data

Glaser, Linda.
   Our big home: an earth poem / by Linda Glaser; illustrated by Elisa Kleven.
       p.   cm.
       Summary: Describes the water, air, soil, sky, sun, and more shared by all living creatures on Earth.
   ISBN 978-0-7613-1650-3 (lib. bdg. : alk. paper)
   ISBN 978-0-7613-1776-0 (pbk. : alk. paper)
   ISBN 978-0-7613-8445-8 (eBook)
       [1. Earth—Fiction. 2. Nature—Fiction.] I. Kleven, Elisa, ill. II. Title.
   PZ7.G48047   Ou   2000
   [E]—dc21   99-045775

Manufactured in the United States of America
11 – PC – 9/1/13

We all live here.
People, ants, elephants, trees,

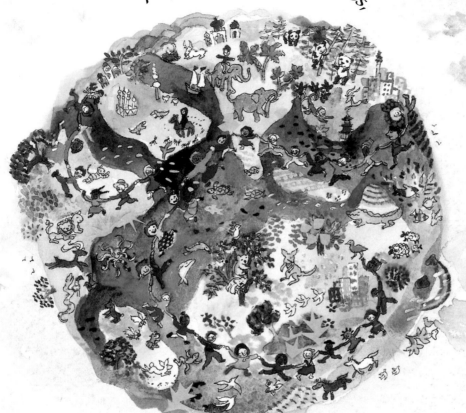

lizards, lichen, turtles, bees.
We all share the same big home.

We share the water.
We splash and slosh and swim in water.
And, of course, we all drink water.
Whales, dolphins, manatees,
penguins, palm trees, you and me.
We all share the water, here on Earth,
our big blue home.

Rain slides down my nose
and trickles in between my toes.
Rain cleans the whole world.
It waters forests of giant trees
and wakes up life in tiny seeds.
It brings fresh water to you and me.
We all share the rain, here on Earth,
our green, growing home.

The sun warms us all,
around the world.
Sunflowers, sparrows, apple trees,
foxes, ferns, and you and me.
Warm fingers and toes,
warm roots and leaves.
We all share the sun, here on Earth,
our big sun-warmed home.

And there's dirt all around,
our earth, our ground.
Soil where seeds wait
and where trees are born,
where earthworms live and rabbits dig.
Earth that holds life,
dirt that feels good under my feet.
We all share the soil, here on Earth,
our big life-holding home.

And there's air everywhere,
far, far away, and right next door.
We all breathe Earth's air. Ahhh. . . .
Doesn't it feel good to breathe?
People, lizards, ladybugs,
oak trees, sweet peas, even weeds.
We all share the air, here on Earth,
our big fresh-air home.

Wind whooshes and whirls
and sweeps and swirls.
It stirs the grass and shakes the trees.
It carries rain and spreads new seeds.
It brings fresh air. It blows kids' hair.
All around the world.
Wind touches us all, here on Earth,
our big whirling home.

The sky,
our huge changing picture up there.
I love our sky. Don't you?
Great sweeps of blue,
dabs and swirls of clouds,
wild splashes at sunset.
Wherever we are,
we look up and see sky, sky, sky.
Here on Earth, our big home
under the sky.

The night,
when stars sparkle
in the deep, endless deep,
the hushed time
when we sink into sleep,
when night animals roam,
and night flowers bloom.
We all have a time of darkness,
here on Earth, our home
under the big blanket
of night.

And our moon travels
across the sky, a creamy pearl,
a thin white sail. Full moon, new moon,
shaping our night. We all share the moon,
here, there, everywhere on Earth,
our big moonlit home.

When I stretch, or dance,
or hop, or laugh,
when I leap in the air or lay in the grass,
I feel alive. We all have that aliveness.
Trees, frogs, bees, grass,
spiders, snakes, earthworms, bats.
We all share life, every one of us,
here on Earth,
our big life-giving home.

We share air, water, soil, sky,
sun, rain, and being alive.

And we all share one home, here on Earth.

One precious living home.